More Soul Retreats

_____

Presented To

_____

Presented By

_____

Date

More Soul Retreats™ for Women
ISBN 0-310-80188-5

Copyright 2003 by GRQ Ink, Inc.
Franklin, Tennessee 37067
"Soul Retreats" is a trademark owned by GRQ, Inc.

Published by Inspirio™, The gift group of Zondervan
5300 Patterson Avenue, SE
Grand Rapids, Michigan 49530

Requests for information should be addressed to:
Inspirio™, The gift group of Zondervan
Grand Rapids, Michigan 49530

http://www.inspiriogifts.com

Editor and Compiler: Lila Empson
Associate Editor: Janice Jacobson
Project Manager: Tom Dean
Manuscript written by Vicki J. Kuyper in conjunction with Snapdragon Editorial Group, Inc.
Design: Whisner Design Group

More
Soul Retreats
for Women

inspirio™

Contents

Introduction

Time for yourself. Time to think, time
to grow, time to find out what lies inside
you. Experts say that's what everyone
needs. But where do you find the time for searching, cleansing, and
refreshing your soul in the middle of your busy day?

More Soul Retreats™ *for Women* continues the tradition of *Soul
Retreats*™ *for Women* and provides a variety of new retreats—pick-
me-ups for your soul as you go about the busyness of your life.
These thirty retreats show you how to capture a little time for
yourself by opening your eyes to simple ways to replenish your
inner resources through such activities as music, poetry, reading,
and prayer.

Browse through the retreat titles each day and choose the
selection that interests you, or simply read the retreats in the order
they appear. Either way, you will discover encouragement,
strength, and insight directed specifically to you as a woman.

The Happy Kingdom in Myself

I do not ask for any crown
But that which all may win;
Nor try to conquer any world
Except the one within.
Be thou my guide until I find,
Led by a tender hand,
The happy kingdom in myself
And dare to take command.

Louisa May Alcott

Take Me Away

A Moment to Pause Stop what you're doing—at least inside your head—and take a few minutes right where you are to enjoy a little time off by exercising your imagination. Close your eyes and let your thoughts carry you to a sandy beach, waves lapping at your feet, a refreshing breeze blowing in off the water.

Focus on the way the wet sand feels between your toes and how the sun warms your skin. Or see yourself near the snowy top of an awesome slope, riding your skis back and forth down the mountain through perfect white powder. Can you feel yourself moving unimpeded, breathing in the chilled air?

Every woman needs to get away from time to time to refuel emotionally. Your thoughts are powerful, and they can take you anywhere you want to go. You can choose where your thoughts take you. It could be to a store filled with rare books or on a train traveling through the desert. Your imaginary destination can be as unique as you are. Perhaps you'd like to go to an artist colony to try your hand at sketching; perhaps you'd enjoy visiting Le Condon Bleu in Paris to learn new cooking techniques. Give yourself the break you need to get you through your day and bring refreshment to your soul.

The soul is dyed the color of its leisure thoughts.
—W. R. INGE

A Moment to Reflect

God used his imagination to create this marvelous universe and all that is in it. That ability to think creatively, to direct your thoughts and to make them work for you, is one of the many abilities he gave you when he created you in his own image.

When you need a lift to help you meet the demands of your day, ask God to accompany you for a refreshing change of scenery. Walk along the beach with him. Share your heart with him as the two of you stand on the mountaintop looking down on the winter white below. It will be good—for you and for all those who depend on you.

To the quiet mind all things are possible. What is the quiet mind? A quiet mind is one which nothing weighs on, nothing worries, which, free from ties and from all self-seeking is wholly merged into the will of God and dead to its own.

☙

—MEISTER ECKHART

9

Be transformed by the renewing of your minds, so that you may discern what is the will of God.

Romans 12:2 NRSV

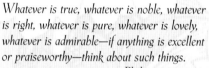

A Moment to Refresh

Whatever is true, whatever is noble, whatever is right, whatever is pure, whatever is lovely, whatever is admirable—if anything is excellent or praiseworthy—think about such things.

Philippians 4:8 NIV

We are destroying speculations and every lofty thing raised up against the knowledge of God, and we are taking every thought captive to the obedience of Christ.

2 Corinthians 10:5 NASB

"My thoughts are not your thoughts, neither are your ways my ways," declares the LORD. "As the heavens are higher than the earth, so are my ways higher than your ways and my thoughts than your thoughts."

Isaiah 55:8–9 NIV

Our life is what our thoughts make it.

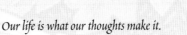

—SAINT CATHERINE OF SIENA

Think of Jesus, whom God sent to be the High Priest of the faith we profess.
Hebrews 3:1 GNT

On my bed I remember you; I think of you through the watches of the night.
Psalm 63:6 NIV

Cast all your anxiety on him because he cares for you.
1 Peter 5:7 NIV

I will remember the deeds of the LORD; yes, I will remember your miracles of long ago. I will meditate on all your works and consider all your mighty deeds.
Psalm 77:11–12 NIV

My thoughts are my company; I can bring them together, select them, detain them, dismiss them.

—WALTER SAVAGE LANDOR

Living Together

Energize your soul by taking a few minutes to settle back and reflect on the family God has given you. Perhaps you can picture your sister's face and the childhood game you loved to play with her. Or it might be the image of your son's sparkling eyes as he said "I love you" for the first time without prompting. Focus on your family's faces and the happy times you've spent with each one. Remember the faces of people who touched your life and are now gone.

Your family members are gifts from God meant to be treasured and appreciated here on earth. They love you, stand up for you, and fill your heart with unspeakable joy. Most of all they make you feel connected to the human race. They provide you with a sense of identity and a place to belong. Consider ways to continue the family traditions they passed down to you. Cherish the memory of grandparents and parents, special aunts and uncles.

As you focus on the good times—laughs, hugs, unique family activities—thank God for making it all possible, for bringing you together and keeping you together through the good times and the not-so-good times. Thank God also for those people who seem like family, those people he has placed in your life to bless you.

Loving relationships are a family's best
protection against the challenges of the world.
—BERNIE WIEBE

A Moment to Reflect

The concept of family is one of God's own making. Throughout the pages of the Bible he consistently demonstrates his commitment to the family unit and family life. So committed is he that he has made it possible through his beloved Son, Jesus, for you to become part of his family.

As you spend time thinking about your earthly family and all they mean to you, thank God for inviting you into the greatest family of all—the family of God. What could be more refreshing to the human soul than to know that you are God's own child?

There's no vocabulary
For love within a family,
Love that's lived in
But not looked at,
Love within the light of which
All else is seen,
The love within which
All other love finds speech.
This love is silent.

❧

—*T. S. ELIOT*

Many waters cannot quench love; rivers cannot wash it away.

Song of Solomon 8:7 NIV

A Moment to Refresh

All the ends of the earth will remember and turn to the LORD, and all the families of the nations will bow down before him.

Psalm 22:27 NIV

He settles the barren woman in her home as a happy mother of children. Praise the LORD.

Psalm 113:9 NIV

Ascribe to the LORD, O families of the peoples, Ascribe to the LORD glory and strength.

Psalm 96:7 NASB

Cornelius and all his family were devout and God-fearing; he gave generously to those in need and prayed to God regularly.

Acts 10:2 NIV

Other things may change us, but we start and end with family.

₧

—Anthony Brandt

I bow my knees before the Father, from whom every family in heaven and on earth derives its name.
Ephesians 3:14–15 NASB

Lo, children are an heritage of the LORD and the fruit of the womb is his reward. As arrows are in the hand of a mighty man; so are children of the youth.
Psalm 127:3–4 KJV

The children of your servants will live in your presence; their descendants will be established before you.
Psalm 102:28 NIV

May the LORD make you increase, both you and your children.
Psalm 115:14 NIV

Earthly fathers and mothers, husbands, wives, children and earthly friends, are all "shadows." But God is the "substance."

₧

—Jonathan Edwards

Praise Him

A Moment to Pause

Step away for a few minutes from all the earthly things that clamor for your attention and look upward. Praise God for the blessings he has placed in your life—the people you treasure, your health, your home, the food on your table. Nothing lifts a woman's soul more than the simple act of praising God.

When you express your admiration to him in words or actions, you are reconnecting on a deep level with your Creator, through whom you have access to all you could ever want or need. If you are in a place where it is appropriate, speak the words out loud. Hearing the praise words will settle them deeply in your heart.

Now speak words of praise to God for who he is—loving, kind, just, and blameless. Of course your words can never fully encompass the greatness of God. He is greater and more wonderful than any human mind can comprehend. Praise him for those qualities you appreciate most.

When you have finished your praising, linger for a few more moments in God's presence. The Bible says that when God's people praise him, he is always there with them. Let him strengthen and inspire your soul as you wait before him.

You awaken us to delight in your praise; for you
have made us for yourself, and our hearts are
restless until they find their rest in you.
—Saint Augustine of Hippo

A Moment to Reflect

Praising God is to the soul what regular exercise is to the body. It strengthens and invigorates. That isn't only because he happens to be worthy of your praise. It is also because praising God helps you to remember that he is bigger than any situation you may be facing— bigger than any personal failure or frustration you may have experienced.

Take time to praise God. Open your mind and heart and soul to the renewal that only he can give. You will find that one of the greatest consequences of praising God is that you will want to praise him even more, drawing down blessed benefits on yourself each time you do.

Let us, with a gladsome mind,
Praise the Lord, for he is kind:
For his mercies aye endure,
Ever faithful, ever sure.

—JOHN MILTON

17

*O Lord, open my lips, and my mouth will
declare your praise.*

Psalm 51:15 NIV

A Moment to Refresh

*Ascribe to the LORD the glory due his name;
worship the LORD in the splendor of his
holiness.*

Psalm 29:2 NIV

*The LORD is my strength and my shield; my
heart trusts in him, and I am helped. My
heart leaps for joy and I will give thanks
to him in song.*

Psalm 28:7 NIV

*Enter his gates with thanksgiving and his
courts with praise; give thanks to him and
praise his name.*

Psalm 100:4 NIV

*You alone are the LORD . . . You give life to
everything, and the multitudes of heaven
worship you.*

Nehemiah 9:6 NIV

The worship of God is not a rule of safety—it is an adventure of the spirit.

๛

—ALFRED NORTH WHITEHEAD

Sing to him, sing praise to him; tell of all his wonderful acts. Glory in his holy name; let the hearts of those who seek the LORD rejoice.
Psalm 105:2–3 NIV

Praise the LORD. Give thanks to the LORD, for he is good; his love endures forever.
Psalm 106:1 NIV

I praise you because I am fearfully and wonderfully made; your works are wonderful, I know that full well.
Psalm 139:14 NIV

I will bless the LORD at all times; His praise shall continually be in my mouth.
Psalm 34:1 NASB

Worship is the celebration of life in its totality.

๛

—WILLIAM STRINGFELLOW

Letting It Go

A Moment to Pause   Carrying around anger and resentment weighs more heavily on your mind and soul than five pounds of cellulite does on your thighs. So give your heart a break. Sit down at your desk and write a letter to someone you need to forgive. Write out all your angry thoughts and feelings, every offense and slight. Tell that person exactly how you feel. Don't leave out a thing.

When you've got it all down on paper, place your hands on the paper and open your heart. Ask God to help you cross over to forgiveness. Then as an act of faith, write a final paragraph to your letter. Express that you are choosing to forgive and that God is helping you to bring your thoughts and emotions into line with that choice. When you're finished, thank God for helping you. End by ripping the letter into small pieces and tossing it in the trash.

Forgiving someone from the heart takes time. You may have to go to God more than once, asking for the strength to let go of deep-seated resentment and to experience true healing. But forgiveness is God's specialty. With his help, it can become yours, as well.

A person's ability to forgive is in proportion to
the greatness of his soul.
—AUTHOR UNKNOWN

A Moment to Reflect

Don't wait for apologies, reconciliation, or even understanding. Make the first move toward forgiveness. Holding on to resentment is like gorging on junk food because someone else called you "fat." All you end up doing is hurting yourself. So let it go and lose that heavy feeling you've been carrying around.

Like losing weight of any kind, forgiving from the heart is hard work. You may be looking at a pile of letters before you've really worked through your feelings. But it's worth it. Once again, you'll be free to laugh, to love, to enjoy life. And the lighthearted, invigorated, refreshed feeling in your soul is the first benefit.

Endeavor to be always patient of the faults and imperfections of others; for thou hast many faults and imperfections of thine own that require forbearance. If thou art not able to make thyself that which thou wishest, how canst thou expect to mold another in conformity to thy will.

—*Thomas à Kempis*

Jesus said, "If you forgive men when they sin against you, your heavenly Father will also forgive you."

Matthew 6:14 NIV

A Moment to Refresh

Be kind to one another, tender-hearted, forgiving each other, just as God in Christ also has forgiven you.

Ephesians 4:32 NASB

Bear with each other and forgive whatever grievances you may have against one another. Forgive as the Lord forgave you.

Colossians 3:13 NIV

Peter came to Jesus and asked, "Lord, how many times shall I forgive my brother when he sins against me? Up to seven times?" Jesus answered, "I tell you, not seven times, but seventy-seven times."

Matthew 18:21–22 NIV

Humanity is never so beautiful as when praying for forgiveness, or else forgiving another.

—JEAN PAUL RICHTER

Jesus prayed, "Forgive us our sins, just as we also have forgiven those who sin against us."

Matthew 6:12 NIRV

Jesus said, "When you stand praying, if you hold anything against anyone, forgive him, so that your Father in heaven may forgive you your sins."

Mark 11:25 NIV

Jesus said, "Do not judge, and you will not be judged. Do not condemn, and you will not be condemned. Forgive, and you will be forgiven."

Luke 6:37 NIV

The only true forgiveness is that which is offered and extended even before the offender has apologized and sought it.

—SÖREN KIERKEGAARD

Quiet Within

A Moment to Pause

Clutter, clamor, and distractions are as much a part of a woman's life as breathing. Appointments, deadlines, meetings, family responsibilities, emergency trips to the grocery or drugstore, clothes to be washed. But there's a quiet spot waiting to be found inside you this very minute—a tiny, tranquil glimpse of heaven you can visit even if your feet are currently planted in a mountain of dirty laundry.

Getting there begins with dropping your worries, like laundry into a hamper, at God's feet. Big or small, legitimate or obsessive, every concern of yours is a concern of his. Close your eyes and take several deep breaths, releasing any tension in your neck and shoulders. Then, picture yourself sitting quietly in God's presence. This is no illusion. He's there.

Next, take an unencumbered mental stroll through the streets of heaven with Jesus by your side. While your mind isn't capable of knowing what that would really be like, you can be sure that it will be an experience filled with absolute peace—the peace only God can give. Bask in it. Enjoy a taste, if just for a moment, of what it means for your soul to be truly at rest.

What peace and inward quiet should he have
who would cut away from himself all busyness
of mind, and think only on heavenly things.
—THOMAS À KEMPIS

A Moment to Reflect

Experiencing peace in a chaotic world isn't natural—it's supernatural. God's peace bears little resemblance to what the world promises will soothe your worried heart and soul. That's because God's peace doesn't depend on favorable circumstances. It prevails no matter what's going on in the world around you with your kids, your job, your husband, or your heart.

Bring much-needed relief to your soul by understanding that God is always with you, waiting to apply his peace to each situation. And the peace he makes available to you here on earth is but a foretaste of what you will experience one day in heaven.

Drop thy still dews of quietness,
Till all our strivings cease;
Take from our souls the strain and stress,
And let our ordered lives confess
The beauty of thy peace.

—JOHN GREENLEAF WHITTIER

God is not a God of disorder but of peace.
1 Corinthians 14:33 NIV

A Moment to Refresh

A heart at peace gives life to the body.
Proverbs 14:30 NIV

You, LORD, give perfect peace to those who keep their purpose firm and put their trust in you.
Isaiah 26:3 GNT

May the Lord of peace Himself continually grant you peace in every circumstance.
2 Thessalonians 3:16 NASB

The LORD gives strength to his people; the LORD blesses his people with peace.
Psalm 29:11 NIV

Love and faithfulness meet together; righteousness and peace kiss each other.
Psalm 85:10 NIV

The time of business does not differ from the time of prayer; and in the noise and clutter of my kitchen, while several persons are at the same time calling for different things, I possess God in as a great tranquility as if I were upon my knees at the Blessed Sacrament.

～

—BROTHER LAWRENCE

The peace that Christ gives is to guide you in the decisions you make; for it is to this peace that God has called you together in the one body.

Colossians 3:15 GNT

Our citizenship is in heaven.

Philippians 3:20 NRSV

We look forward to possessing the rich blessings that God keeps for his people. He keeps them for you in heaven, where they cannot decay or spoil or fade away.

1 Peter 1:4 GNT

Pray for the peace of Jerusalem: "May those who love you be secure. May there be peace within your walls and security within your citadels."

Psalm 122:6–7 NIV

O God, make us children of quietness and heirs of peace.

～

—SAINT CLEMENT OF ROME

Slowing Your Steps

A Moment to Pause Do you start running from the moment your alarm sounds and you roll out of bed in the morning—running car pools, running to the office, running to grab some lunch, running errands, and in the process, running yourself ragged? Think how good it would feel to slow yourself down to a comfortable walk—for your soul's sake.

So take five. Whether it's five minutes, five blocks, or five miles, get out your prettiest pair of athletic shoes. And as you put them on, use that action as a reminder to invite God to join you. As you get under way, breathe deeply and slowly. Focus on your heart beating, your lungs filling with air, and the muscles in your legs contracting. Thank God for the wonder of being a woman.

As you begin to hit your stride, listen to the sounds around you—the song of the birds on the fence, the laughter of children, the excited pants of the dogs playing in the sun. Notice the details—the warm breeze on your face, the flower growing in the crack of the sidewalk, the scent of bread as you pass a bakery. Let every step you take soothe your soul.

Thoughts come clearly while one walks.
—*Thomas Mann*

A Moment to Reflect

God wants to walk with you through your daily life just as he walks with you on the sidewalk in front of your house, or on a tree-lined walking trail, or on an old dirt road. He wants to walk with you through the good times and the difficult times, on rainy days and sunny days. God is kind and gentle. He's waiting for you to ask him to come along with you.

Walk through life sharing each step with the one who created it all. Open your heart and ask him in. Your soul will thank you for it.

Walk quietly—

And know that He is God.

When the dawn on winged steed comes riding high,

To blazon painted banners on the morning sky,

When evening shadows lie against the hill—

In the hush of twilight, when the world is still.

Walk quietly.

—Author Unknown

In your heart you plan your life. But the LORD decides where your steps will take you.

Proverbs 16:9 NIRV

A Moment to Refresh

Moses said: These commandments that I give you today are to be upon your hearts. Impress them on your children. Talk about them when you sit at home and when you walk along the road, when you lie down and when you get up.

Deuteronomy 6:6–7 NIV

What does the LORD require of you but to do justice, and to love kindness, and to walk humbly with your God?

Micah 6:8 NRSV

Very early in the morning, while it was still dark, Jesus got up, left the house and went off to a solitary place, where he prayed.

Mark 1:35 NIV

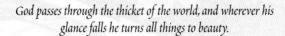

*God passes through the thicket of the world, and wherever his
glance falls he turns all things to beauty.*

—SAINT JOHN OF AVILA

*Whether you turn to the right or to the left,
your ears will hear a voice behind you,
saying, "This is the way; walk in it."*
Isaiah 30:21 NIV

*The man and his wife heard the sound of
the LORD God as he was walking in the
garden in the cool of the day.*
Genesis 3:8 NIV

*I will walk among you, and will be your
God, and you shall be my people.*
Leviticus 26:12 NRSV

*Make level paths for your feet and take
only ways that are firm.*
Proverbs 4:26 NIV

*Climb the
mountains and get
their good tidings.
Nature's peace will
flow into you as
sunshine flows into
trees. The winds
blow their freshness
into you, and the
storms their energy,
while cares will drop
off like falling
leaves.*

—JOHN MUIR

Rejoicing Always

A Moment to Pause

Kids know how to find happiness in unexpected places. An empty box, fallen leaves, a puddle of mud . . . Want to feel like a kid again? Blow bubbles. If your home is beyond the bubble solution stage, fill a small saucer with dishwashing liquid and fashion a paper clip into a loop. Dip the paper clip into the solution, then lift and blow.

See how far you can blow the bubbles across the room. Watch how quickly they pop. Note their color and size. Try and outdo yourself for the biggest bubble or the most bubbles created in one blow.

Now, dip a little deeper into your soul. Sure, it's fun to blow bubbles. But happiness is as fleeting as the bubbles you're blowing. Joy, however, is something that is infinitely more sturdy than a fragile film of soap. It's something that bubbles up from your soul regardless of season or circumstance.

As you blow bubbles, reflect on times of true joy in your life, such as the birth of a child, an intimate time of worship, or a surprising answer to prayer. Ask God to show you how to nurture a deeper joy in your daily life.

There is not one blade of grass, there is no color in the world that is not intended to make us rejoice.
—JOHN CALVIN

A Moment to Reflect

The one universal action you can take that will help fill your soul and your life with joy is to know God. The better you get to know him through reading the Bible, praying, doing what you believe he is leading you to do, and seeing him work in the lives of your friends and family, the more joy you'll discover you have and be able to share.

Joy is the result—the reward—of becoming reconnected to the one who created you, the one who loves you and gave his life for you. In his presence you will find fullness of joy.

As the hand is made for holding and the eye for
seeing, you have fashioned me, O Lord, for joy.
Share with me the vision to find joy everywhere:
in the wild violet's beauty, in the lark's melody, in
the face of a steadfast man, in a child's smile, in a
mother's love, in the purity of Jesus.

—SCOTS CELTIC PRAYER

May my lips overflow with praise, for you
teach me your decrees.

Psalm 119:171 NIV

A Moment to Refresh

A cheerful look brings joy to the heart.

Proverbs 15:30 NIRV

Rejoice evermore. Pray without ceasing. In
every thing give thanks: for this is the will of
God in Christ Jesus concerning you.

1 Thessalonians 5:16–18 KJV

Shout with joy to God, all the earth!

Psalm 66:1 NIV

The LORD is my strength and my shield; my
heart trusts in him, and I am helped. My heart
leaps for joy and I will give thanks to him in
song.

Psalm 28:7 NIV

Sing to the LORD a new song; play skillfully,
and shout for joy.

Psalm 33:3 NIV

Joy is the surest sign of the presence of God.

—PIERRE TEILHARD DE CHARDIN

You will face all kinds of trouble. When you do, think of it as pure joy. Your faith will be put to the test. You know that when this happens it will produce in you the strength to continue.

James 1:2–3 NIRV

As a bridegroom rejoices over his bride, so will your God rejoice over you.

Isaiah 62:5 NIV

This is the day which the LORD hath made; we will rejoice and be glad in it.

Psalm 118:24 KJV

Let all who take refuge in you, O LORD, be glad; let them ever sing for joy. Spread your protection over them, that those who love your name may rejoice in you.

Psalm 5:11 NIV

We are all strings in the concert of his joy; the spirit from his mouth strikes the note and the tune of our strings.

—JAKOB BOEHME

Soul Review

A Moment to Pause

Life is the soul's classroom. And today it's time to review what you've learned. Take out your appointment book or journal and review what the last twelve months have brought your way. Think of the relationships that have entered your life. Reflect on the victories, as well as the challenges, you've faced. Then, take out a sheet of paper and write down what you've discovered about yourself, about God, and about those who have been around you in the past year. In what ways have you become a better woman?

When you've finished writing, reread what you've written. Take time to thank God for the confident person he's helping you become. Praise him for his lessons. Ask him for help in areas where you could use a little extra tutoring.

When you're finished, write "soul review" on next year's calendar, one year from today's date. Finish by putting today's paper in a safe place, where you can review it next year. It will serve as a reminder of how far you've come.

Teachers know the importance of reviewing and testing students on what they've learned. They know this process helps plant information and skills more firmly in students' minds. As a student of life, reviewing what you've learned will keep your soul from growing stagnant, leading you toward growth and maturity.

Anyone who keeps learning stays young.
—Henry Ford

A Moment to Reflect

Spiritual learning has many benefits and rewards. A soul that continues to grow by learning something new is a soul that's vibrantly alive. It's one that approaches life with wonder, a thirst for knowledge, and a desire to grow that can be described as eager— eager to grow in faith, eager to approach life, eager to learn, and eager to mature.

When God reveals something in your life that needs to change, embrace it with enthusiasm. Make a point to learn and grow. Becoming the woman God created you to be is a day-by-day, year-by-year process of which learning is an integral part.

Take your needle, my child,
and work at your pattern;
it will come out a rose by and by.
Life is like that;
one stitch at a time taken patiently,
and the pattern will come out all right,
like embroidery.

—OLIVER WENDELL HOLMES

Let the wise listen and add to their learning.
Proverbs 1:5 NIV

A Moment to Refresh

Continue in the things you have learned and become convinced of, knowing from whom you have learned them.
2 Timothy 3:14 NASB

Being wise is better than being strong; yes, knowledge is more important than strength.
Proverbs 24:5 GNT

Whatever you have learned or received or heard from me, or seen in me—put it into practice. And the God of peace will be with you.
Philippians 4:9 NIV

Let the wise listen and add to their learning, and let the discerning get guidance—for understanding proverbs and parables, the sayings and riddles of the wise.
Proverbs 1:5–6 NIV

Learning is not attained by chance. It must be sought for with ardor and attended to with diligence.

꒯

—*ABIGAIL ADAMS*

Don't live any longer the way this world lives. Let your way of thinking be completely changed.

Romans 12:2 NIRV

Grow in the grace and knowledge of our Lord and Savior Jesus Christ.

2 Peter 3:18 NRSV

Skill will bring success.

Ecclesiastes 10:10 NIV

Anything you say to the wise will make them wiser. Whatever you tell the righteous will add to their knowledge. To be wise you must first have reverence for the LORD. If you know the Holy One, you have understanding.

Proverbs 9:9–10 GNT

Life is the soul's nursery—its training place for the destinies of eternity.

꒯

—*WILLIAM MAKEPEACE THACKERAY*

Line by Line

A Moment to Pause

A good novel can get your adrenaline going, leading you to turn pages faster and faster. Poetry can have the opposite effect. It slows you down. It makes you stop, think, question, and reflect. Take a poetry break right now.

Begin by reading Psalm 143:5–6: "I remember the days of long ago; I meditate on all your works and consider what your hands have done. I spread out my hands to you; my soul thirsts for you like a parched land. *Selah*" (NIV).

This may not look like the poetry you're accustomed to. It doesn't include measured stanzas or patterns of rhyme. But the Psalms are filled with the poetic expression of raw emotion and metaphor. They were originally written to be sung as a form of worship. That's why some of them include musical terms, like *selah*.

Selah means pause. During this pause, people would listen to a musical interlude or simply reflect on what had been sung. *Selah* was a kind of soul retreat written directly into the poem. So, *selah* right now. Reread the words above. Picture yourself as a solitary woman in a parched land. How does God quench your thirst? Stop, think, question, reflect, and pray. A prayer is a poem with wings.

Poetry is the spontaneous overflow of powerful feelings: it takes its origin from emotion recollected in tranquility.
— WILLIAM WORDSWORTH

A Moment to Reflect

Reading through Psalms on your own is one way to immerse yourself in great poetry, at the same time working a little selah into your daily schedule. If you read a psalm a day, you will have three months worth of prayer-provoking poetry before you finish the book.

Try reading one each morning—before putting on your makeup. This will remind you to be the real you when you talk to God, the way the psalmists were. Pay attention to the emotions expressed in each psalm and the honesty with which they are voiced, whether joy, anger, despair, or praise. Don't forget to selah as you read.

Could we with ink the ocean fill,
And were the heavens of parchment made,
Were every stalk on earth a quill,
And every man a scribe by trade,
To write the love of God above
Would drain the ocean dry,
Nor could the scroll contain the whole,
Though stretch'd from sky to sky.

— "Chaldee Ode," translated by
Rabbi Mayir ben Isaac

Like the pen of a good writer my tongue is ready with a poem.

Psalm 45:1 GNT

A Moment to Refresh

He put a new song in my mouth, a hymn of praise to our God.

Psalm 40:3 NIV

An idea well-expressed is like a design of gold, set in silver.

Proverbs 25:11 GNT

You are my hiding place. You will keep me safe from trouble. You will surround me with songs sung by those who praise you. Selah

Psalm 32:7 NIRV

My heart overflows with a beautiful thought! I will recite a lovely poem to the king, for my tongue is like the pen of a skillful poet.

Psalm 45:1 NIV

The psychological mechanism used by grace to raise us to prayer
is the same that puts in movement the poetic experience.

—HENRI BREMOND

Trust in him at all times, O people; pour out your hearts to him, for God is our refuge. Selah

Psalm 62:8 NIV

You, O LORD, are a shield around me, my glory, and the one who lifts up my head. I cry aloud to the LORD, and he answers me from his holy hill. Selah

Psalm 3:3–4 NRSV

Who is he, the King of glory? The Lord Almighty— he is the King of glory. Selah

Psalm 24:10 NIV

Miriam sang this song: "I will sing to the LORD, for he has triumphed gloriously; he has thrown both horse and rider into the sea."

Exodus 15:21 NIV

One drop of God's strength is worth more than all the world.

—DWIGHT L. MOODY

Flexing Your Muscles

A Moment to Pause   When trying to gain physical strength, you go to the gym. When trying to strengthen your soul, you go to God. Do it now. Ask him to reveal your areas of strength and weakness. Praise him for any strengths that may come naturally. Ask for insight into how to use your strengths in a way that will cause others to praise him instead of you.

Take a close, honest look at your weaknesses. This is the first step in creating a personal workout program to strengthen your character as well as your soul. As any personal trainer will tell you, building strength doesn't happen overnight. It takes repeated exercise focused on specific areas. Choose one specific area now. Then choose an exercise that will turn this flabby feature into pure muscle.

For instance, if fear holds you back from exercising your faith, find a scripture that reminds you of God's protection. Memorize that verse and repeat it to yourself every time the butterflies in your stomach take flight. If you're struggling with a quick temper, practice holding your tongue long enough to think wisely before speaking rashly whenever you get irritated. Getting your soul in shape takes practice, patience, and perseverance. The benefits last a lifetime.

A poem is the very image of life expressed in its eternal truth.

—PERCY BYSSHE SHELLEY

A Moment to Reflect

As any woman who works out regularly at the gym can testify, having a workout partner can keep you going when you'd rather throw in the towel. The same is true for your spiritual workout. Ask a close friend to be an accountability partner. Choose someone you trust implicitly and respect spiritually. Then dare to bare your weaknesses.

Give your friend permission to ask you how your exercise program is progressing. Ask her to share any additional areas of weakness she may see in your life. Be vulnerable enough, and humble enough, to accept both criticism and praise. Praying together will strengthen this relationship, as well as both your souls.

"As the day thy strength shall be!"
This should be enough for thee;
He who knows thy frame will spare
Burdens more than thou canst bear.
When thy days are veiled in night,
Christ shall give thee heavenly light;
Seem they wearisome and long,
Yet in Him thou shalt be strong.

—Frances Ridley Havergal

March on, my soul; be strong!

Judges 5:21 NIV

A Moment to Refresh

"I am strong and will save them. My name is The LORD Who Rules Over All."

Jeremiah 50:34 NIRV

It is God who arms me with strength and makes my way perfect.

2 Samuel 22:33 NIV

I can do all things through Him who strengthens me.

Philippians 4:13 NASB

I love you, LORD; you are my strength. The LORD is my rock, my fortress, and my savior; my God is my rock, in whom I find protection. He is my shield, the strength of my salvation, and my stronghold.

Psalm 18:1–2 NIV

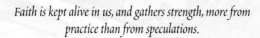

Faith is kept alive in us, and gathers strength, more from practice than from speculations.

ॐ

—JOSEPH ADDISON

The LORD is my strength and my might, and he has become my salvation.
Exodus 15:2 NRSV

The joy of the LORD is your strength.
Nehemiah 8:10 NRSV

I am well content with weaknesses, with insults, with distresses, with persecutions, with difficulties, for Christ's sake; for when I am weak, then I am strong.
2 Corinthians 12:10 NASB

The godly will flourish like palm trees and grow strong like the cedars of Lebanon. For they are transplanted into the LORD's own house. They flourish in the courts of our God.
Psalm 92:12–13 NIV

We must always change, renew, rejuvenate ourselves; otherwise we harden.

ॐ

—JOHANN WOLFGANG VON GOETHE

Affirming the Good

A Moment to Pause   Pause for a moment and think about the women who have consistently been an encouragement to you, either through their words, their actions, or their example. One might be a family member or close friend who has been there for you during difficult times. Another could be someone you worked with who urged you forward in your career. Still another might be someone who has encouraged you in your relationship with God.

As each person comes to your mind, pause and picture her standing before you. Reflect on the specific ways she has encouraged you. Did her quirky sense of humor cheer you? Did her wise advice enable you to solve a dilemma or make a difficult decision? Did you want to become the type of woman that she modeled for you? Thank God for that person.

After you've spent some time remembering these wonderful women, refresh their souls in return. Write a brief note to each woman, thanking her for the way she encouraged you. Tell each one how you see God's image brightly reflected in her life, and mention what you have learned about the gift of encouragement from her godly example. In the process, you will undoubtedly encourage her in return.

Encouragement is oxygen to the soul.
—GEORGE M. ADAMS

A Moment to Reflect

Every characteristic you appreciate in the individuals who mean the most to you is a reflection of God's character. It's a glimpse of God that draws you to him when you feel that spark of love, friendship, and encouragement in others.

When people in your life do something to encourage your soul, don't just make a point of thanking them. Thank God for the beauty of his own perfect character shining through them. Meditate on the characteristic that most deeply touches your heart at the moment. Then ask for the wisdom and strength to more fully develop that characteristic in your own life.

Make it a rule, and pray to God to help you keep it, never, if possible, to lie down at night without being able to say: "I have made one human being at least a little wiser, or a little happier, or at least a little better this day."

—CHARLES KINGSLEY

He who refreshes others will himself be refreshed.

Proverbs 11:25 NIV

A Moment to Refresh

Let us consider how to stimulate one another to love and good deeds, not forsaking out own assembling together, as is the habit of some, but encouraging one another; and all the more as you see the day drawing near.

Hebrews 10:24–25 NASB

Encourage one another and help one another, just as you are now doing.

1 Thessalonians 5:11 GNT

May our Lord Jesus Christ himself and God our Father, who loved us and by his grace gave us eternal encouragement and good hope, encourage your hearts and strengthen you in every good deed and word.

2 Thessalonians 2:16–17 NIV

Praise, like gold and diamonds, owes its value only to its scarcity.

෴

—SAMUEL JOHNSON

We urge you, our friends, to warn the idle,
encourage the timid, help the weak, be
patient with everyone.
                    1 Thessalonians 5:14 GNT

Encourage one another daily, as long as it
is called Today, so that none of you will be
hardened by sin's deceitfulness.
                    Hebrews 3:13 NIV

A word aptly spoken is like apples of gold
in settings of silver.
                    Proverbs 25:11 NIV

Jonathan went to find David and
encouraged him to stay strong in his faith
in God.
                    1 Samuel 23:16 NIV

*Encouragement
costs you nothing to
give, but it is
priceless to receive.*

෴

—AUTHOR
UNKNOWN

Taking a Bow

A Moment to Pause The Olympic Games only take place every four years, but you can take your soul on a trip to the winner's platform right now. Cheering fans fill the stadium. A trumpet fanfare sounds in the air. A massive torch burns brightly nearby. And there you are on the highest platform, awaiting the gold.

Now think back over your life and consider when you've deserved a gold medal. It could be in any one or more of the roles you play: friend, mother, wife, employee, child of God. When have your efforts exceeded your own expectations? When have you kept going, even when the odds were not in your favor? What accomplishments have given you the greatest pleasure? When have you given your all?

Picture a gold medal being placed around your neck for each of these victories. Listen to the national anthem playing in your honor. Celebrate the satisfaction of a job well done.

When it comes to daily life, you have this same opportunity, with or without the fanfare. One significant difference is that though it may feel like you're in competition with the rest of the world, in reality God's placed you in a solo event. No one can achieve the will of God for your life, except you.

The applause of a single human being is of
great importance.
—SAMUEL JOHNSON

Praise and accolades are great motivators. So is applause from those around you. Even more important, however, is the applause of the One who made you. The moments in your life that make God proud may look very different from the ones that came to your mind as being medal worthy, but they are worth celebrating even more.

When you achieve something noteworthy in your life, whether publicly or privately, make a point of inviting God to the victory party. Every one of your accomplishments is a joint effort—God supplies you with talents and opportunities, and your job is to follow through with passion and perseverance.

I do not ask for any crown
But that which all may win;
Nor try to conquer any world
Except the one within.
Be thou my guide until I find,
Led by a tender hand,
The happy kingdom in myself
And dare to take command.

—LOUISA MAY ALCOTT

*Each will be rewarded according to his own
labor. For we are God's fellow workers.*
                                    1 Corinthians 3:8–9 NIV

A Moment to Refresh

*Charm is deceptive and beauty disappears, but
a woman who honors the LORD should be
praised. Give her credit for all she does. She
deserves the respect of everyone.*
                                    Proverbs 31:30–31 GNT

*The quality of each person's work will be seen
when the Day of Christ exposes it. For on that
Day fire will reveal everyone's work; the fire
will test it and show its real quality.*
                                    1 Corinthians 3:13 GNT

*God's gifts of grace come in many forms. Each
of you has received a gift in order to serve
others. You should use it faithfully.*
                                    1 Peter 4:10 NIRV

*We have different gifts, according to the grace
given us.*
                                    Romans 12:6 NIV

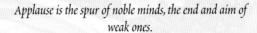

Applause is the spur of noble minds, the end and aim of weak ones.

၁

—CHARLES CALEB COLTON

Whatever you do, work at it with all your heart, as though you were working for the Lord and not for people.

Colossians 3:23 GNT

God is not unjust; he will not overlook your work and the love that you showed for his sake in serving the saints, as you still do.

Hebrews 6:10 NRSV

If one of you wants to be great, you must be the servant of the rest.

Mark 10:43 GNT

Boaz said to Ruth, "May you be richly rewarded by the LORD, the God of Israel, under whose wings you have come to take refuge."

Ruth 2:12 NIV

Let us work as if success depended on ourselves alone, but with the heartfelt conviction that we are doing nothing and God everything.

၁

—SAINT IGNATIUS OF LOYOLA

Bubbles, Bubbles Everywhere

A Moment to Pause Begin your day with a bubble bath. Grab a quick half-hour soak during your lunch hour. Schedule time in the tub on a Saturday afternoon. Or substitute watching the evening news for basking in bubbles glistening by candlelight.

Why wait until nightfall? Take a little private time, right now. The house is finally quiet. When it comes to relaxation and soul restoration, time in the tub is well spent. Light a solitary candle and slip into something more comfortable—a tub filled with warm, soothing water topped with a froth of fragrant bubble bath, beads, salts, or oil. Then just step in.

If finding at least thirty uninterrupted minutes isn't possible at the moment, enjoy a "dry run." Lie down on the couch or your bed. Close your eyes and imagine the sound of running water, the sweet floral scent of your favorite bath fragrance, and lots of bubbles. Picture the bubbles multiplying as the water rises. Slip into that tub in your mind. Feel the warm water caress your body as a stray bubble tickles your nose. Breathe deeply as you feel your muscles relax, and cares dissolve. Reflect on how feeling clean on the outside makes you feel on the inside.

With joy you will draw water from the wells of salvation.

—ISAIAH 12:3 NRSV

A Moment to Reflect

One of the beauties of a bubble bath is that you can get clean without scrubbing. In the same way, a squeaky clean soul isn't something you have to work at. Inner purity is a gift from God who has done a work of grace on your behalf.

Whenever you take a bath, make sure you are clean both inside and out. As you soak, spend a few moments confessing to God any areas where you feel you have fallen short. Then, bask in the warm comfort of God's cleansing forgiveness. As you drain the tub, picture all of the wrong choices you've made going down the drain along with the dirty water. Enjoy the blessing of being wholly clean.

Oh! To be clean as a mountain river!
Clean as the air above the clouds,
or on the middle seas!
As the throbbing ether that fills the gulf
between star and star!
Nay, as the thought of the Son of Man Himself.

—George MacDonald

Remove my sin, and I will be clean; wash me,
and I will be whiter than snow.

Psalm 51:7 GNT

A Moment to Refresh

When the kindness and love of God our Savior
appeared, he saved us, not because of righteous
things we had done, but because of his mercy.
He saved us through the washing of rebirth and
renewal by the Holy Spirit.

Titus 3:4–5 NIV

Let us draw near to God with a sincere heart in
full assurance of faith, having our hearts
sprinkled to cleanse us from a guilty conscience
and having our bodies washed with pure water.

Hebrews 10:22 NIV

Jesus said, "First clean the inside of the cup, so
that the outside may become clean."

Matthew 23:26 NRSV

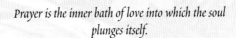

Prayer is the inner bath of love into which the soul plunges itself.

—Jean-Baptiste Marie Vianney

Do not call anything impure that God has made clean.

Acts 10:15 NIV

Above all else, guard your heart, for it is the wellspring of life.

Proverbs 4:23 NIV

When you look into water, you see a likeness of your face. When you look into your heart, you see what you are really like.

Proverbs 27:19 NIRV

I wash my hands to declare my innocence. I come to your altar, O LORD, singing a song of thanksgiving and telling of all your miracles.

Psalm 26:6–7 NIV

Plenteous grace with Thee is found, grace to cover all my sins; let the healing streams abound, make and keep me pure within.

—Charles Wesley

Plugged In

A Moment to Pause   Take a few minutes to do some maintenance checkup on your spiritual connection. Do a brief inventory of what you do to keep connected to God. Do you pray? Study your Bible? Journal your blessings? Read an inspirational bestseller? Reach out to others with God's love? Act on what you believe God wants you to do? All these actions are good for boosting energy and maintaining your spiritual resources.

The idea of a checkup is to forestall any potential problems. In any area where you feel there could be a future problem, figure out now how you can avoid it. Write down your solution. Make a list, if necessary. Choose one thing on your list that you can do right this minute. Then just do it. Pray, journal, pick up your Bible, or make that phone call. Afterward, reflect on how you feel more empowered as a woman and as a child of God by taking that one small step.

God wired everyone, including capable women like you, to work hand in hand with him. You can guarantee an eventual power outage if you try to pull off life on your own. The only way to keep the power in your life is to keep the connection with the Source of all power.

We are the wire. God is the current. Our only power is to let the current pass through us.
—CARLO CARRETTO

A Moment to Reflect

One way to assure you're spiritually grounded is to get plugged into a local church. That means showing up on Sunday to hear someone speak—but it also means preparing your heart to learn from what you hear. It means being authentic with the people you meet, developing relationships, and joining together for prayer and praise. It means sharing your resources—your time, treasure, and talents. It may even mean getting involved in a Bible study, helping out in the nursery, or singing in the choir.

Whatever becoming actively involved in a church community may mean to you, it will help strengthen your connection to God as well as recharge your soul.

The spacious firmament on high
With all the blue ethereal sky,
And spangled heavens, a shining frame,
Their great original proclaim:
The unwearied sun, from day to day,
Does his Creator's power display,
And publishes to every land
The work of an almighty hand.

—JOSEPH ADDISON

61

God used his power to make the earth. His wisdom set the world in place. His understanding spread the heavens out.

Jeremiah 10:12 NIRV

A Moment to Refresh

God has said to me, "My grace is sufficient for you, for power is perfected in weakness." Most gladly therefore, I will rather boast about my weaknesses, so that the power of Christ may dwell in me.

2 Corinthians 12:9 NASB

God's divine power has given us everything needed for life and godliness, through the knowledge of him who called us by his own glory and goodness.

2 Peter 1:3 NRSV

The prayer of a godly person is powerful. It makes things happen.

James 5:16 NIRV

*Confidence should arise from beneath,
and power descend from above.*

ॐ

—EMMANUEL JOSEPH SIEYÉS

*Praise God in his sanctuary; praise him in
his mighty heavens. Praise him for his acts
of power; praise him for his surpassing
greatness.*

Psalm 150:1–2 NIV

*You will receive power when the Holy
Spirit has come upon you.*

Acts 1:8 NRSV

*To him who by means of his power working
in us is able to do so much more than we
can ever ask for, or even think of: to God
be the glory in the church and in Christ
Jesus for all time, forever and ever!*

Ephesians 3:20–21 GNT

*There is no limit to
the power of a good
woman.*

ॐ

—ROBERT HUGH
BENSON

Focusing on God

A Moment to Pause

Meditating on scripture is a great way to focus on God. Begin by reading one Bible verse. Take "God is love" (1 John 4:16) for starters. Close your eyes and think about the words individually. What picture does the word God bring to mind? What emotions and experience?

Next think about the word is. Is may seem insignificant at first. Yet consider how the fact that God "is"—that he exists, that he's present, that he has no beginning or end—affects your life? How does the fact that "God is" affect your eternity? Now think about the word love. What type of actions does love bring to mind? How have you seen an invisible God's love visibly at work in the world?

After you've spent a few minutes thinking about each word individually, concentrate on what they mean as a unit. Repeat the words quietly to yourself. What does God is love mean to you? What does the phrase say about God? How does thinking about this scripture draw you closer into God's presence? How does it bring God's character more clearly in focus?

Some other verses that are good for this kind of meditation include "Love never fails" (1 Corinthians 13:8), "Love one another" (John 15:12), and "Blessed are the peacemakers" (Matthew 5:9).

Let us leave the surface and, without leaving the world, plunge into God.

—PIERRE TEILHARD DE CHARDIN

A Moment to Reflect

This soul retreat focuses on a type of meditation called lectio divina, which is Latin for "divine reading." This method of focusing on God by meditating on scripture has been used for hundreds of years.

While it's important to read larger sections of the Bible to fully understand the context of a verse and get the big picture of God's Word, biting off one small chunk at a time will help focus your thoughts on a specific idea, really seeing details you might have missed while reading the larger passage. Take time to linger over a single scripture and meditate on it. Each time you do, you will gain new insight about God.

It is no use to ask what those who love God do with Him.
There is no difficulty in spending our time with a friend we love;
our heart is always ready to open to Him;
we do not study what we shall say to Him,
but it comes forth without premeditation;
we can keep nothing back—
even if we have nothing special to say,
we like to be with Him.

—FRANÇOIS FÉNELON

Within your temple, O God, we meditate on
your unfailing love.

Psalm 48:9 NIV

A Moment to Refresh

I remember the days of old, I think about all
your deeds, I meditate on the works of
your hands.

Psalm 143:5 NRSV

Fill your minds with those things that are good
and that deserve praise: things that are true,
noble, right, pure, lovely, and honorable.

Philippians 4:8 GNT

Set your minds on things above, not on
earthly things.

Colossians 3:2 NIV

Help me understand the meaning of your
commandments, and I will meditate
on your wonderful miracles.

Psalm 119:27 NIV

Devout meditation on the Word is more important to soul-health even than prayer. It is more needful for you to hear God's words than that God should hear yours, though the one will always lead to the other.

&

—FREDERICK BROTHERTON MEYER

Jesus said, "You shall love the Lord your God with all your heart, and with all your soul, and with all your strength, and with all your mind."

Luke 10:27 NRSV

Do not let this Book of the Law depart from your mouth; meditate on it day and night, so that you may be careful to do everything written in it.

Joshua 1:8 NIV

Let the words of my mouth, and the meditation of my heart, be acceptable in thy sight, O LORD, my strength, and my redeemer.

Psalm 19:14 KJV

Meditation is like a needle after which comes a thread of gold, composed of affections, prayers and resolutions.

&

—SAINT ALPHONSUS

Aromas from the Kitchen

A Moment to Pause

Fresh bread baking in the oven, steak and onions sizzling on the grill, coffee brewing merrily—every woman knows that food is more than just nourishment for the body. It's also a feast for her senses and her soul. Fix yourself a small snack right now. Make sure that whatever mini-repast you prepare combines at least two ingredients. The menu can be as simple as a piece of toast with jelly or a cup of hot tea with lemon and honey.

Taste each ingredient separately as you prepare your snack. Then sit down and enjoy the finished culinary combination. Resist the temptation to read the paper, chat on the phone, or even gaze out the window. Savor every bite. Pay attention to the texture, the temperature, the aroma. Think of the unique taste you're experiencing. Consider how different the ingredients taste once they are combined.

Thank God for the wonderful experience he designed to accompany the simple act of being nourished. Praise him for the wide variety of flavors and textures he has provided to please your palate. From artichokes to zucchini, relishing the smorgasbord God has set before you can make every meal a potential soul retreat. Just sit down and enjoy.

The discovery of a new dish does more for the
happiness of mankind than the discovery of a star.
—ANTHELME BRILLAT-SAVARIN

A Moment to Reflect

In the Old Testament, God provided manna for the Israelites to eat when their food ran scarce in the desert. It not only filled their stomachs, but it also had a honeylike taste to please their palates. God has shown the same care for you. Not only has he made food for you to eat, but he has also provided a wide variety of pleasing choices.

Before you begin your meal, bow your head for a moment and let God know you are genuinely grateful for what he has so generously provided—food that not only satisfies your hunger but also satisfies your soul.

We may live without poetry, music and art;
We may live without conscience,
And live without heart;
We may live without friends;
We may live without books;
But civilized man cannot live without cooks.

—*Edward Robert Bulwer-Lytton*

69

*Whether you eat or drink or whatever you do,
do it all for the glory of God.*

1 Corinthians 10:31 NIV

A Moment to Refresh

*I will bless you as long as I live; I will lift up
my hands and call on your name. My soul is
satisfied as with a rich feast, and my mouth
praises you with joyful lips.*

Psalm 63:4–5 NRSV

Jesus prayed, "Give us today the food we need."

Matthew 6:11 GNT

*How sweet are your words to my taste, sweeter
than honey to my mouth!*

Psalm 119:103 NRSV

*I, the LORD your God . . . would feed you with
the best of foods. I would satisfy you with wild
honey from the rock.*

Psalm 81:10, 16 NIV

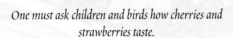

*One must ask children and birds how cherries and
strawberries taste.*

ॐ

—Johann Wolfgang von Goethe

Jesus said, "I am the living bread that came
down from heaven. If anyone eats of this
bread, he will live forever."

John 6:51 NIV

God said, "Everything that lives and moves
will be food for you. I have already given
you the green plants for food. Now I am
giving you everything."

Genesis 9:3 NIRV

O taste and see that the LORD is good.

Psalm 34:8 KJV

O God, you satisfy me more than the
richest of foods. I will praise you with
songs of joy.

Psalm 63:5 NIV

*Know that even
when you are in the
kitchen, our Lord
moves amidst the
pots and pans.*

ॐ

—Saint Teresa of
Avila

Furry Friends

A Moment to Pause A close encounter of the furry kind can be a great boost for your soul. Think back to when you were a little girl and recall the animals that graced your life. Perhaps it was a personal pet, the pooch next door, or the lion at the zoo. Think back to what it was about that critter that made you smile. What did it do, look like, or feel like that warmed your heart? Which of its unique characteristics intrigued you, comforted you, or amused you?

If you have the privilege of currently sharing your home with a pet, take a break right now and spend some quality time. Take your pet in your arms (unless, of course, it's a goldfish), and hold it close. Experience how relaxing its rhythmic breathing or purring can be. Stroke its fur or fluff its feathers. How does your pet let you know it loves you? Tell your pet, and God, what you enjoy most about it.

Then treat your pet to some playtime or a favorite treat. Chances are you will both come away feeling refreshed and invigorated. Connecting with one of God's creatures can be both relaxing and rewarding, a unique balm for to refresh your soul.

All animals except man know that the principle
business of life is to enjoy it.
—SAMUEL BUTLER

A Moment to Reflect

When God created animals, he put them under the care of humans. While it's true he created them to assist the human race, the sheer magnitude and magnificence of the animal kingdom makes it reasonable to think that perhaps he created them for man's enjoyment, as well.

Even the most reluctant animal lover can easily see and appreciate what God has created in the animal kingdom. The diversity and details are incredible examples of God's handiwork. God created every creature with care and proclaimed it "good." So be sure to thank him for each one that passes through your life.

He prayeth best, who loveth best
All things both great and small;
For the dear God who loveth us,
He made and loveth all.

—SAMUEL TAYLOR COLERIDGE

God gives animals their food and feeds the
young ravens when they call.

Psalm 147:9 GNT

A Moment to Refresh

God commanded, "Let the earth produce all
kinds of animal life: domestic and wild, large
and small"—and it was done. So God made
them all, and he was pleased with what he saw.

Genesis 1:24–25 GNT

How many are your works, O LORD! In
wisdom you made them all; the earth is full of
your creatures.

Psalms 104:24 NIV

LORD, your constant love reaches the heavens;
your faithfulness extends to the skies . . . People
and animals are in your care.

Psalm 36:5–6 GNT

I would give nothing for that man's religion whose very dog and cat are not the better for it!

⤳

—ROWLAND HILL

God tends his flock like a shepherd: He gathers the lambs in his arms and carries them close to his heart; he gently leads those that have young.

Isaiah 40:11 NIV

Praise God, all you wild animals and cattle. Praise him, you small creatures and flying birds.

Psalm 148:10 NIRV

Don't you know who made everything? Haven't you heard about him? The LORD is the God who lives forever. He created everything on earth.

Isaiah 40:28 NIRV

Every single creature is full of God and is a book about God.

⤳

—MEISTER ECKHART

Bowing Before Him

A Moment to Pause   God answers prayer, and every prayer has an answer, though sometimes it may go unrecognized. Encourage your soul with the gift of recognizing and giving thanks for answered prayers. Begin by recalling some of the things you've prayed for during the past year, and place an empty jar and a pile of coins on the kitchen table while you're having your first cup of coffee.

Now reflect on these questions: Were the answers what you expected? Are there some answers you're still waiting for? Are you now glad that God answered "no" to some of your prayers? Ask God to bring to mind requests you may have forgotten you prayed. Place a coin in the jar with a prayer of thanksgiving each time you recognize God's answer to a specific petition.

The Bible describes how a pile of stones was used as a reminder of God's faithfulness. When God stopped the Jordan River so the Israelites could cross safely, stones from the dry riverbed were gathered into a pile on the opposite bank. This memorial helped future generations remember God's miraculous answer to prayer.

When your retreat is complete, leave the jar on the table and encourage others to contribute coins to acknowledge their answered prayers.

There are four ways God answers prayer: No,
not yet; No, I love you too much; Yes, I thought
you'd never ask; Yes, and here's more.

—ANNE LEWIS

A Moment to Reflect

Having a visual reminder of God's faithfulness—whether a jar of coins, an answered-prayer scrapbook, or even a pile of rocks in the backyard—can be a great encouragement to your faith. This reminder serves as evidence that God cares about you and your concerns personally, and keeping your reminder in a visible location will remind you daily.

Each time you pass the kitchen table and see your jar sitting there, pause for a moment and thank God for all he has done for you and for those you love. When the jar is full, use the coins to answer someone else's prayer.

New mercies, each returning day,
Hover around us while we pray;
New perils past, new sins forgiven,
New thoughts of God, new hopes of heaven.

—JOHN KEBLE

Devote yourselves to prayer, being watchful and thankful.

Colossians 4:2 NIV

A Moment to Refresh

All people will come to you, because you hear and answer prayer.

Psalm 65:2 NIRV

The LORD said, "Before they call I will answer; while they are still speaking I will hear."

Isaiah 65:24 NIV

Jesus said, "Whatever you ask for in prayer with faith, you will receive."

Matthew 21:22 NRSV

The LORD has heard my plea; the LORD will answer my prayer.

Psalm 6:9 NIV

I love the LORD because he hears and answers my prayers. Because he bends down and listens, I will pray as long as I have breath!

Psalm 116:1–2 NIV

We pray for silver, but God often gives us gold instead.

૪

—MARTIN LUTHER

The Lord said, "Call to me and I will answer you and tell you great and unsearchable things you do not know."
Jeremiah 33:3 NIV

LORD, hear my prayer! In your righteousness listen to my plea; answer me in your faithfulness!
Psalm 143:1 GNT

In the morning, O LORD, you hear my voice; in the morning I lay my requests before you and wait in expectation.
Psalm 5:3 NIV

We will fulfill our vows to you, O God, for you answer our prayers, and to you all people will come . . . You faithfully answer our prayers with awesome deeds, O God our savior. You are the hope of everyone on earth.
Psalm 65:1–2, 5 NIV

God never denied that soul anything that went as far as heaven to ask for it.

૪

—JOHN TRAPP

A Wing and a Prayer

A Moment to Pause

The Bible says that God takes care of the birds of the air. Take a moment to gaze out the window over your kitchen sink or the one behind your office desk, wherever you have a good view of the birds flying about outside.

Watch as they seem to glide effortlessly on the soft air currents and skip joyfully on the ground. Listen to their delighted chirping and cheerful songs. Notice how they appear to rest free of all care in the branches of the trees, on the roofs of houses, and on the telephone lines. Feast your eyes on their marvelous shapes and colors. Imagine how it must feel to be one of them, completely committed to God's care and trusting him to meet your every need.

Jesus said to observe the birds of the air and see how God takes care of them (Matthew 6). Then he said that you are of much greater value to God than the birds, and wouldn't he watch over you and provide for your needs just as faithfully as he does theirs?

Reflect on that truth for a moment. Then let your imagination take flight. Picture yourself as free as a bird, secure in the care of your heavenly Father.

No ladder needs the bird but skies to situate its
wings, nor any leader's grim baton arraigns it
as it sings.

—EMILY DICKINSON

A Moment to Reflect

You may be one of those people who find it difficult to trust God for your needs because you believe he expects you to take care of yourself. God does expect you to do your part. He expects you to behave responsibly and obey his commandments, just as he expects the birds to seek out the food he has sprinkled about for them and fly south to avoid the cold weather.

Still there are probably many things in your life that you can't manage on your own. For those things, he asks that you trust in him. When you do, you will find that your soul is once again able to fly.

All things bright and beautiful,
all creatures great and small,
all things wise and wonderful,
the Lord God made them all.
Each little flower that opens,
each little bird that sings,
he made their glowing colors,
he made their tiny wings.

—CECIL FRANCES ALEXANDER

Hide me under the shadow of thy wings.
Psalm 17:8 KJV

A Moment to Refresh

The LORD shielded Jacob, cared for him, guarded him as the apple of his eye. As an eagle stirs up its nest, and hovers over its young; as it spreads its wings, takes them up, and bears them aloft on its pinions, the LORD alone guided him.
Deuteronomy 32:10–12 NRSV

God said, "Let the water teem with living creatures, and let birds fly above the earth across the expanse of the sky."
Genesis 1:20 NIV

Jesus said, "Look at the birds: they do not plant seeds, gather a harvest and put it in barns; yet your Father in heaven takes care of them! Aren't you worth much more than birds?"
Matthew 6:26 GNT

*The little singing birds sang of God, the animals acclaimed him,
the elements feared and the mountains resounded with him, the
rivers and springs threw glances toward him,
the grasses and flowers smiled.*

—JOHN CALVIN

*What are human beings, that you think of
them; mere mortals that you care for them?*
Psalm 8:4 GNT

*Come, let us bow down and worship him;
let us kneel before the LORD, our Maker!
He is our God; we are the people he cares
for, the flock for which he provides.*
Psalm 95:6–7 GNT

Homes are made by the wisdom of women.
Proverbs 14:1 GNT

*Those who hope in the LORD will renew
their strength. They will soar on wings like
eagles.*
Isaiah 40:31 NIV

*The birds of the air nest by the waters; they
sing among the branches.*
Psalm 104:12 NIV

*My soul was always
so full of
aspirations, that a
God was a necessity
to me. I was like a
bird with an instinct
of migration upon
me, and a country
to migrate to was as
essential as it is to
the bird.*

—HANNAH WHITALL
SMITH

Breaking Out

A Moment to Pause   Some celebrations take place in the quietest of moments to honor the simplest of victories. Take time for that kind of celebration right now. Find a comfortable spot—and bring along a candle.

Before you strike the match, choose the theme for your celebration. It could simply be the start of a brand-new day. Perhaps it's the completion of a project at work, the risk you took in confronting a friend, the gift of your child finally sleeping through the night, or a milestone in your quest to become a woman of godly character.

As you light your candle, say a prayer of thanks to God for the event you are celebrating, for his resources and favor employed on your behalf, and for the people who helped to make it possible. Then lift your hands and your voice in worship to God. Let your emotions flow freely—laughing, weeping, singing, shouting—until your soul once again becomes quiet within you.

Before you blow out your candle, consider how you can carry the joy of your celebration with you throughout your day. Present someone special with a rose to celebrate another day of friendship. Surprise your kids with balloons to celebrate God's gift of them to you. Celebrate the victory God enabled you to accomplish.

> *All our life is a celebration for us; we are convinced, in fact, that God is always everywhere.*
> —CLEMENT OF ALEXANDRIA

A Moment to Reflect

After God created the world, he took a day off to rest and to celebrate what he'd done. The beginning of each new day presents the same opportunity to you. Today is filled with fresh opportunities and brand-new blessings, and God has never created another twenty-four hours just like it.

Getting in the habit of celebrating the little things as well as the big things will help you become more aware of how priceless every day is, how extraordinary, how praiseworthy. For your soul's sake, follow God's example. Look around you and acknowledge that what you have accomplished with God's help is good.

The soul of one who loves God
always swims in joy,
always keeps holiday,
and is always in a mood for singing.

—SAINT JOHN OF THE CROSS

There's a time to laugh. There is a time to be
sad. And there's a time to dance.

Ecclesiastes 3:4 NIRV

A Moment to Refresh

Nehemiah said, "Go and enjoy choice food and
sweet drinks, and send some to those who have
nothing prepared. This day is sacred to our
Lord."

Nehemiah 8:10 NIV

Rejoice in the Lord always; again I will say,
rejoice!

Philippians 4:4 NASB

The whole assembly then agreed to celebrate the
festival seven more days; so for another seven
days they celebrated joyfully.

2 Chronicles 30:23 NIV

One generation will commend your works to
another; they will tell of your mighty acts . . .
They will celebrate your abundant goodness and
joyfully sing of your righteousness.

Psalm 145:4, 7 NIV

In seed time learn, in harvest teach, in winter enjoy.

—William Blake

Better is one day in your courts than a thousand elsewhere.

Psalm 84:10 NIV

You have changed my sadness into a joyful dance; you have taken away my sorrow and surrounded me with joy.

Psalm 30:11 GNT

As a groom is delighted with his bride, so your God will delight in you.

Isaiah 62:5 GNT

One generation will commend your works to another; they will tell of your mighty acts . . . They will celebrate your abundant goodness and joyfully sing of your righteousness.

Psalm 145: 4, 7 NIV

The holiest of holidays are those kept by ourselves in silence and apart; the secret anniversaries of the heart.

—Henry Wadsworth Longfellow

Touching Lives

A Moment to Pause   You know firsthand that your soul needs regular times of retreat. Strengthening your soul changes you inside and inspires you to reach out. Try putting yourself empathically in another's shoes. Pick up the morning paper and read the front page for a few minutes. Read it not as news but as stories of individuals loved by God.

Picture yourself as the mother trying to care for her family in the face of famine, the stockholder who has lost her entire savings through the underhanded dealings of management, the wife whose husband has died in a military training exercise. How do you feel? What would you do next? What do you need from others? What do you long for from God?

Pray for all those you've read about. Prayer is one way of touching lives that are far removed from your own. But don't stop there. Resolve to open your eyes to the needs around you. It's not your job to solve the world's problems, but you can make a difference in the lives of some. And that's all God asks from you—that you do your part to help those in need and to make the world a better place.

A cheerful heart does not count the cost of what
he gives. His heart is set on pleasing and
cheering him to whom the gift is given.
—Julian of Norwich

A Moment to Reflect

You are the hands and feet of an invisible God. While God has the power to miraculously heal a broken heart or supply a basic need, he usually uses people, just like you, to make his love visible to a hurting world.

An observant soul is a tender soul. Trying to be more sensitive to the needs that surround you, and becoming more aware of the material, physical, and spiritual gifts God has given you helps you mature into someone else's answer to prayer waiting to be used. Risk reaching out. Let God work through you to help others.

Have you had a kindness shown? Pass it on;
'Twas not given for thee alone, Pass it on;
Let it travel down the years,
Let it wipe another's tears,
'Til in Heaven the deed appears—Pass it on.

૩

—Henry Burton

Share with God's people who are in need.
Practice hospitality.

Romans 12:13 NIV

A Moment to Refresh

Whoever is kind to the poor lends to the LORD,
and will be repaid in full.

Proverbs 19:17 NRSV

If you serve, you should do it with the strength
God provides. Then in all things God will be
praised through Jesus Christ.

1 Peter 4:11 NIRV

A kindhearted woman gains respect.

Proverbs 11:16 NIV

Surely goodness and love will follow me all the
days of my life, and I will dwell in the house of
the LORD forever.

Psalm 23:6 NIV

A kind heart is a fountain of gladness, making everything in its vicinity freshen into smiles.

◇

—WASHINGTON IRVING

Blessed is the person who is kind to those in need.

Proverbs 14:21 NIRV

Rejoice with those who rejoice, and weep with those who weep.

Romans 12:15 NASB

Whenever you possibly can, do good to those who need it.

Proverbs 3:27 GNT

Our Lord's divine power has given us everything we need for life and godliness through our knowledge of him who called us by his own glory and goodness.

2 Peter 1:3 NIV

You will find, as you look back upon your life, that the moments that stand out are the moments when you have done things for others.

◇

—HENRY DRUMMOND

Getting Rid of Clutter

A Moment to Pause

You can find freedom and refreshment in clearing clutter. So today, instead of pondering, you're going to be purging your possessions. Head for your bedroom closet. While you're checking it out, ask God for joy in the job ahead. Pray for wisdom in deciding what to let go of and what to hold on to. Then start the sorting process.

As you gather clothes you no longer need or no longer wear—the dress that's too big, the sweater that's too tight, the robe you haven't worn in a year, the shoes that don't match any of your clothes—think of each item as a stone you're preparing to skim across a mountain lake. Don't just drop your clothes into a pile, toss them with a flick of your wrist several feet away.

Imagine the sound of each stone breaking the water's surface. Picture the ripples emanating from its point of entry across the lake toward your feet. Before continuing, enjoy the soothing image of your stone sinking to its watery resting place.

Then carefully fold each of your discards and place them into a bag to donate to charity. Enjoy the breathing room you've made in your closet and your soul. Feel the freedom of having fewer rocks cluttering up your life.

Clutter is what happens to things when they become useless but friendly.

RUSSELL LYNES

A Moment to Reflect

Every item of clothing comes with a price. That price has to do with money, of course, but the price is also that of time and attention. The more you have to take care of and the more clutter that fills your life, the less time, energy, and resources you have to give to other things. Purchasing, laundering, dusting, shopping, scrubbing, repairing, and discarding are simply more commitments to squeeze into your busy schedule.

Keep it simple. At least twice a year, ask God for wisdom in getting rid of any "stones" you've accumulated. The less clutter you have to care for, the less there will be to distract you from the more important things in life.

Whatever we have of this world in our hands,
our care must be to keep it
out of our hearts,
lest it come between us and Christ.

✍

—MATTHEW HENRY

*There is a time for everything . . . a time to
keep and a time to throw away.*
Ecclesiastes 3:1, 6 NIV

A Moment to Refresh

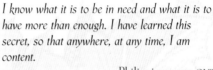

*I know what it is to be in need and what it is to
have more than enough. I have learned this
secret, so that anywhere, at any time, I am
content.*
Philippians 4:12 GNT

*Godliness with contentment is great gain. For
we brought nothing into this world, and it is
certain we can carry nothing out.*
1 Timothy 6:6–7 KJV

Homes are made by the wisdom of women.
Proverbs 14:1 GNT

*The wisdom that comes from heaven is first of
all pure; then peace–loving, considerate,
submissive, full of mercy and good fruit,
impartial and sincere.*
James 3:17 NIV

Simplicity is making the journey of this life with just baggage enough.

჻

—CHARLES DUDLEY WARNER

Keep your lives free from the love of money and be content with what you have.
Hebrews 13:5 NIV

Jesus said, "Be on your guard against wanting to have more and more things. Life is not made up of how much a person has."
Luke 12:15 NIRV

As goods increase, so do those who consume them. And what benefit are they to the owner except to feast his eyes on them?
Ecclesiastes 5:11 NIV

You will be made rich in every way so that you can be generous on every occasion, and through us your generosity will result in thanksgiving to God.
2 Corinthians 9:11 NIV

The ability to simplify means to eliminate the unnecessary so that the necessary may speak.

჻

—HANS HOFMANN

With Love from Me to You

A Moment to Pause   Writing a letter is a wonderful way to express your love and concern for another person. The recipient may be someone who lives around the block or around the world. She may be a longtime friend or a person who has especially blessed your life.

Take out a sheet of paper, an informal note, or—if you feel a long dissertation coming on and if your handwriting may be difficult to read—sit down at your computer. If you choose to type instead of handwrite your letter, be sure to send it via regular mail rather than email. You want to bless your friend with something she can hold in her hands and reread when her heart needs a hug.

Take a moment to pray for the person you are about to write. Then let your loving message flow. Emphasize the things you love about your friend. Enjoy the feelings of caring that pass through you as you choose words of encouragement and support.

Don't rush as you write. Let your sincerity and friendship dictate every line. When you are finished, seal your letter with a prayer for God's blessing on your friend. Send your letter on its way with thanks to God for this relationship.

More than kisses, letters mingle souls; for thus friends absent speak.
—JOHN DONNE

A Moment to Reflect

Expressing how much you care for someone by putting your feelings into words is an act of love that feeds your soul as well as the recipient's. God performed this same act of love with his own love letter, the Bible. Much of the New Testament was written as letters to friends and churches, as God inspired each author. The word epistle, in fact, means personal, handwritten correspondence.

So, as you read the Bible, think of it as God's personal note to you. Why do you think God included what he did for you to read? What kind of response do you think this love letter is asking for?

With fond affection true,
I write these lines for you;
By this token you may see,
I still remember thee.

ک

—MARY F. TRAVER

I always thank my God when I remember you in my prayers.

Philemon 4 NIRV

A Moment to Refresh

John wrote: I have much to write to you, but I do not want to use paper and ink. Instead, I hope to visit you and talk with you face to face, so that our joy may be complete.

2 John 1:12 NIV

Pleasant words are like a honeycomb, sweetness to the soul and health to the body.

Proverbs 16:24 NRSV

Like cold water to a weary soul is good news from a distant land.

Proverbs 25:25 NIV

My heart is stirred by a noble theme as I recite my verses for the king; my tongue is the pen of a skillful writer.

Psalm 45:1 NIV

When you receive a letter from a friend, you should not hesitate to embrace it as a friend.

Ⅼ

—SAINT ISIDORE OF SEVILLE

I have written to you briefly, exhorting and testifying that this is the true grace of God.
1 Peter 5:12 NASB

The righteous person is a guide to his friend.
Proverbs 12:26 GNT

Worry can rob you of happiness, but kind words will cheer you up.
Proverbs 12:25 GNT

All the believers here send greetings. Greet one another with the kiss of peace. With my own hand I write this: Greetings from Paul . . . My love be with you all in Christ Jesus.
1 Corinthians 16:20, 24 GNT

No distance of place or lapse of time can lessen the friendship of those who are thoroughly persuaded of each other's worth.

Ⅼ

—ROBERT SOUTHEY

God's Fairest Blossom

A Moment to Pause

Find yourself a flower. It could be a single iris from an arrangement on your dining room table or a rose growing in your own garden. It could even be a pesky dandelion that has sprouted at the end of your driveway. Hold the flower in your hand. Feel the velvety softness of the petals, the strength of the stem, and the texture of its leaves.

Smell it. Is there a fragrance? Study it. Explore every detail, every curve and line, the color of the blossom and shades of green on the stem and leaves. What makes it beautiful? Is there anything about it that is considered common? If so, what and why?

Consider the creative hand that fashioned it, the very same hand that fashioned you. Take a look in the mirror. Explore every detail, every curve and line of your own face. How has God made it beautiful? How is it different from those around you? Is there anything about it you consider common? If so, what and why?

Take a moment with God. Tell him, from the depths of your soul, how you feel about the face he has created for you. Then sit quietly and listen for God's response. He longs for you to fully know and enjoy what a beautiful woman you are.

Flowers are the sweetest things that God ever made, and forgot to put a soul into.
—HENRY WARD BEECHER

A Moment to Reflect

While television and magazines push a narrow view of beauty, every one of God's creations reflects his glory. This indescribable beauty has nothing to do with the right hair color or a wrinkle-free complexion. The beauty that God created defies comparison. What is more beautiful, after all, a cheetah or a sunset? An orchid or an ocean shore?

Learning to appreciate God's workmanship and unique image as reflected in yourself, others, and the world around you is a soother for your soul. It fosters contentment and praise. Viewing yourself as a one-of-a-kind, priceless work of art—and heart—will help you take a peek at yourself through God's eyes. It's a beautiful view.

Turn my soul into a garden, where the flowers dance in the gentle breeze, praising You with their beauty. Let my soul be filled with beautiful virtues; let me be inspired by Your Holy Spirit; let me praise You always.

ॐ

—Saint Teresa of Avila

Our life is like grass. We grow and flourish like a wild flower.

Psalm 103:15 GNT

A Moment to Refresh

Look how the wild flowers grow: they don't work or make clothes for themselves. But I tell you that not even King Solomon with all his wealth had clothes as beautiful as one of these flowers.

Luke 12:27 GNT

See! The winter is past; the rains are over and gone. Flowers appear on the earth; the season of singing has come.

Song of Songs 2:11–12 NIV

The grass withers, the flower fades; but the word of our God will stand forever.

Isaiah 40:8 NRSV

'Tis my faith that every flower enjoys the air it breathes.

ॐ

—WILLIAM WORDSWORTH

Let us go out early to the vineyards, and see whether the vines have budded, whether the grape blossoms have opened and the pomegranates are in bloom.

Song of Songs 7:12 NRSV

The desert will rejoice, and flowers will bloom in the wastelands.

Isaiah 35:1 GNT

Ever since the world was created it has been possible to see the qualities of God that are not seen. I'm talking about his eternal power and about the fact that he is God. Those things can be seen in what he has made.

Romans 1:20 NIRV

Many flowers open to the sun, but only one follows him constantly—Heart, be thou the sunflower, not only open to receive God's blessing, but constant in looking to him.

ॐ

—JEAN PAUL RICHTER

Digging in the Dirt

A Moment to Pause

A simple seed is a storehouse for miracles. Let your soul take an active part in the ongoing wonder of creation by picking up a packet of seeds from a local nursery. Choose something that's hardy and fast growing, such as marigolds, sweet peas, or beans. Read the directions on the packet and then prepare to dig in and get dirt under your fingernails.

As you get ready to plant the seeds in your yard or in a window box, enjoy the smell of the moistened soil. Imagine what the mature plant will look like. Compare that image to the tiny seed in your hand. Does the seed give any clue as to the miracle that lies ahead? After the seeds are planted, sit down and take at least five minutes to think about the growth process.

Compare your soul to the seeds you've just planted. What stage of growth is it in? Is your faith in God still in the freshly planted seed stage? Are there a few fragile green shoots peeking up from the soil? Do your roots go down deep, strengthened by both the sun and storms of life? Take time to ask God what you can do to help care for the seed of faith he's planted in you.

One is nearer God's heart in a garden than anywhere else on earth.
—DOROTHY FRANCES GURNEY

A Moment to Reflect

Growth and change take time. Whether waiting for a plant to sprout in your garden or a seed of faith to come to blossom in your soul, maturity is a slow process. And waiting for that metamorphosis—the first marigold bud or a trust in God that stands fast during hard times—takes patience. You have all you need when you rely on God.

Be patient with yourself and others as you grow. Like watching newly planted seeds, growth isn't always evident to the eye. God knows just the season, and timetable, every soul needs to bring it into full bloom.

We plough the fields, and scatter
The good seed on the land,
But it is fed and water'd
By God's Almighty Hand.

—Ancient Hymn

There is at time to plant. And there's a time to pull up what is planted.

Ecclesiastes 3:2 NIRV

A Moment to Refresh

The LORD said, "I will send you rain in its season, and the ground will yield its crops and the trees of the field their fruit."

Leviticus 26:4 NIV

God said, "I give you every seed-bearing plant on the face of the whole earth and every tree that has fruit with seed in it. They will be yours for food."

Genesis 1:29 NIV

Paul wrote: I planted, Apollos watered, but God gave the growth. So neither the one who plants nor the one who waters is anything, but only God who gives the growth.

1 Corinthians 3:6–7 NRSV

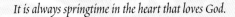

It is always springtime in the heart that loves God.

—JEAN-BAPTISTE MARIE VIANNEY

The LORD God planted a garden in Eden,
in the East, and there he put the man he had
formed. He made all kinds of beautiful trees
grow there and produce good fruit.
Genesis 2:8 GNT

The LORD your God will bless you in all
your harvest and in all the work of your
hands, and your joy will be complete.
Deuteronomy 16:15 NIV

As long as the earth endures, seedtime and
harvest, cold and heat, summer and winter,
day and night, shall not cease.
Genesis 8:22 NRSV

*He who makes a
garden works hand
in hand with God.*

—DOUGLAS
MALLOCH

Inner Longings

A Moment to Pause
It's time to quiet your mind and listen to the longings of your soul. Even if you haven't heard from them in a while, they're still there, painting your dreams and whispering hope into your heart. Find a spot where you can get comfortable, and bring along a pencil and paper. Pay attention to what comes to mind as you ponder the question, What do I long for?

Write down your deepest longings. At first, what you write might seem a little like a Christmas wish list. But delve deeper. Behind that longing for a carpool-free day may be a desire for more personal freedom—or it could be your body's exhausted cry for some extended downtime.

Turn your longing list into a time of prayer. God already knows the deepest desires of your heart. Ask that he would reveal them to you, as well.

Finish by asking God for the courage to hope. It takes a faith-filled heart to keep moving forward with joy while at the same time carrying unfulfilled longings. Be open to God satisfying your longings in unexpected ways in his own time. Then keep your eyes open for his answers to the deepest cries of your soul.

What oxygen is to the lungs, such is hope for the meaning of life.
—HEINRICH EMIL BRUNNER

A Moment to Reflect

The pursuit of happiness cannot meet your deepest desires. Only God can do that. Wealth, success, and popularity may feel satisfying for a while, but people who rely on things like these to fill their longings will never be satisfied ultimately.

In that respect, having unfulfilled longings is a good thing. God uses these longings to point people to him, because at the heart of every deep desire lies a longing for something that only God can give. Knowing you have access to gifts such as unconditional love, forgiveness, peace, and eternal life is the only unshakeable source of hope.

Behind the clouds the starlight lurks,
Through showers the sunbeams fall;
For God, who loveth all His works,
Has left His hope for all.

—JOHN GREENLEAF WHITTIER

Our hope is certain. It is something for the soul to hold on to.

Hebrews 6:19 NIRV

A Moment to Refresh

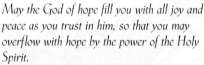

May the God of hope fill you with all joy and peace as you trust in him, so that you may overflow with hope by the power of the Holy Spirit.

Romans 15:13 NIV

I will find my rest in God alone. He is the One who gives me hope.

Psalm 62:5 NIRV

"I know the plans I have for you," declares the LORD, "plans to prosper you and not to harm you, plans to give you hope and a future."

Jeremiah 29:11 NIV

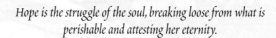

Hope is the struggle of the soul, breaking loose from what is perishable and attesting her eternity.

—HERMAN MELVILLE

Hope does not disappoint, because the love of God has been poured out within our hearts through the Holy Spirit who was given to us.

Romans 5:5 NASB

Faith is being sure of what we hope for and certain of what we do not see.

Hebrews 11:1 NIV

Command those who are rich in the things of this life not to be proud, but to place their hope, not in such an uncertain thing as riches, but in God, who generously gives us everything for our enjoyment.

1 Timothy 6:17 GNT

Hope is faith holding out its hand in the dark.

—AUTHOR UNKNOWN

Hold That Pose

A Moment to Pause

Science fiction is filled with tales of time machines. But in the real world, the only device that can enable you to travel back in time is your memory. With the aid of photographs, you're ready for your journey to begin. Find one of your old photo albums, preferably one you haven't looked at in a while. As you dust off the cover, clear any distractions from your mind, as well. Then sit down, relax, and buckle yourself in for a praise-filled ride.

Take your time as you turn each page. Don't skim the photographs. Relive them. Recall why each snapshot was taken. What made these moments ones that you wanted to hold on to? Let every image—the people you've known and loved, the places you've visited, the things you've enjoyed—inspire you to thank God for one positive memory related to each subject or occasion. Thank God that he was with you then and is with you now.

As you close the album, take a moment to bring yourself back to the present. Ask yourself, If I were to give God a photo of me right now, something I wanted him to treasure, where would I want to be and what would I want to be doing?

A good snapshot stops a moment
from running away.
—EUDORA WELTY

A Moment to Reflect

Photographs are memories you can hold in your hand. But you don't have to have a fancy camera to take a mental snapshot. God's gift of memory automatically creates your own personal scrapbook. And just like taking a good photo, the secret to capturing picture-perfect memories depends on focus.

The proper focus for every memory is seeing life from God's perspective. Keeping God's purposes and presence in mind when looking at the past brings clarity and insight. Memories like this help strengthen your soul by using the past to help you gain a clearer focus on God's hand in the present.

Hold that pose and smile for me . . .
Let's embrace this priceless memory.
Then, for longer than time will allow,
We can celebrate this gift of "now."

&

—CATHRYN ATKINSON

113

The memory of the righteous will be a blessing.
Proverbs 10:7 NIV

A Moment to Refresh

We, who with unveiled faces all reflect the Lord's glory, are being transformed into his likeness with ever–increasing glory, which comes from the Lord, who is the Spirit.
2 Corinthians 3:18 NIV

The LORD does not see as mortals see; they look on the outward appearance, but the LORD looks on the heart.
1 Samuel 16:7 NRSV

Remember the days of old; consider the generations long past.
Deuteronomy 32:7 NIV

I will perpetuate your memory through all generations; therefore the nations will praise you for ever and ever.
Psalm 45:17 NIV

Treat your friends as you do your pictures,
and place them in the best light.

꙳

—JENNIE JEROME CHURCHILL

Smiling faces make you happy.
　　　　　　　Proverbs 15:30 GNT

A happy heart makes the face cheerful.
　　　　　　　Proverbs 15:13 NIV

Your face is lovely.
　　　　　Song of Songs 2:14 NRSV

Timothy has just now come to us from you
and has brought good news about your
faith and love. He has told us that you
always have pleasant memories of us and
that you long to see us, just as we also long
to see you.
　　　　　1 Thessalonians 3:6 NIV

The value of
anything is what the
next day's memory
of it shall be.

꙳

—AUTHOR
UNKNOWN

We Thank You, Lord

A Moment to Pause   Take out a sheet of your best stationery. Or, if you prefer, sit down at your computer. It's time to write a heartfelt thank you note. You won't need any postage, and your spelling won't be checked. This note is headed straight for heaven.

Listing the blessings God has brought into your life from birth to the present would take you a lifetime to write. So limit this note to the number one blessing that comes to mind right now. Even though it's easy to simply say a quick thank–you to God via prayer, your soul can better explore and enjoy the depth of your gratitude if you take the time to write God a note of appreciation in the same way you would write to a friend who touched your heart with unexpected kindness.

Think of how this blessing has changed your life, how it has encouraged your heart, and how it has met an individual need or desire. Consider what your life would be like without it. As you're finishing up, add a paragraph listing the blessings you've been given today—especially those you might easily overlook. Put the finished note into an envelope addressed to My Heavenly Father and keep it in your Bible. Open and read it anytime you are facing a discouraging day.

God is always meeting the needs of all of His children.

—EDWARD MILLER

A Moment to Reflect

When a friend goes out of her way to do something for you, it's natural to thank her and brag to others about what she's done. Think about doing the same thing with God. Freely share what God has done in your life. Your words may help others recognize his hand at work in their own circumstances, as well as encourage them to respond in praise along with you.

Blessings are best shared, both verbally and physically. When God's gifts bring about an abundance of material resources, use them to bless others. It may just be one of the reasons God brought the blessing your way in the first place.

An easy thing, O Power Divine,
To thank thee for these gifts of Thine,
For summer's sunshine, winter's snow,
For hearts that kindle, thoughts that glow;
But when shall I attain to this—
To thank Thee for the things I miss?

—THOMAS WENTWORTH HIGGINSON

The same Lord is Lord of all and richly blesses all who call on him.

Romans 10:12 NIV

A Moment to Refresh

God will fully satisfy every need of yours according to his riches in glory in Christ Jesus.

Philippians 4:19 NRSV

The faithful will abound with blessings.

Proverbs 28:20 NRSV

The LORD gives strength to his people; the LORD blesses his people with peace.

Psalm 29:11 NIV

Blessed are all who fear the LORD, who walk in his ways.

Psalm 128:1–2 NIV

Praise be to the God and Father of our Lord Jesus Christ, who has blessed us in the heavenly realms with every spiritual blessing in Christ.

Ephesians 1:3 NIV

*O Thou who hast given us so much, mercifully grant us one
more thing—a grateful heart.*

—GEORGE HERBERT

*Every good thing given and every perfect
gift is from above, coming down from the
Father of lights, with whom there is no
variation or shifting shadow.*
James 1:17 NASB

*I will send down showers in season; there
will be showers of blessing.*
Ezekiel 34:26 NIV

*Blessings are like crowns on the heads of
those who do right.*
Proverbs 10:6 NIRV

*You will go out in joy and be led forth in
peace; the mountains and hills will burst
into song before you, and all the trees of the
field will clap their hands.*
Isaiah 55:12 NIV

*Now let the soul
number its gains
and count its
treasures. They are
so fine that they
refine the hands
which count them.*

—PHILLIPS BROOKS

Dreaming Big

A Moment to Pause Spiritual bifocals are essential to leading a visionary life. They help you focus clearly both close up (on what is happening now), and far away (on what is yet to happen). Put on a pair right now. Now close your eyes and dare to dream.

First, ground your future dreams in reality. Use those imaginary bifocals to focus closely on where you are right now. Picture your daily routine. Next, ask yourself a few questions: What gives you energy? What depletes your energy? What would you like to change? What areas and abilities would you like to improve? What relationships would you like to make? What relationships would you like to see grow deeper?

Last, change your focus to the future. Picture yourself in five . . . ten . . . twenty . . . thirty . . . forty years. How do you look in your mind's eye? What dreams would like to see come true before you finish your life here on earth? How can you see God using the abilities he's given you in even greater ways than he is now? Is there anything you can do in the present to help you better prepare for the future? Dream big. Dream bold. Dream the impossible. With God, the impossible can happen.

Vision encompasses vast vistas outside the realm
of the predictable, the safe, the expected.
—CHARLES R. SWINDOLL

A Moment to Reflect

When you were a little girl, you may have dreamed of one day becoming a ballerina, an astronaut, or a rock-'n'-roll singer. As you mature, and your soul grows closer to God, your vision for the future changes. You may still long to be a ballerina, but above all, you will long to be the woman God has created you to become—wherever that takes you. That's because in God's eyes, who you are is of greater importance than what you do.

Like any father, God loves to give his children what they long for, although his vision for your life may differ a bit from your own. He knows the desires of your heart.

Vision that looks inward becomes duty.
Vision that looks outward
becomes aspiration.
Vision that looks upward becomes faith.

—AUTHOR UNKNOWN

Delight yourself in the LORD and he will give
you the desires of your heart.

Psalm 37:4 NIV

A Moment to Refresh

Where there is no vision, the people perish.

Proverbs 29:18 KJV

May the LORD give you what your heart longs
for. May he make all your plans succeed.

Psalm 20:4 NIRV

You open your hand and satisfy the desires of
every living thing.

Psalm 145:16 NIV

During the night the mystery was revealed to
Daniel in a vision.

Daniel 2:19 NIV

The angel of God said to me in the dream,
"Jacob." I answered, "Here I am."

Genesis 31:11 NIV

Vision is the art of seeing things invisible.

—JONATHAN SWIFT

Jesus said, "All things are possible with God."

Mark 10:27 NASB

God asked Abraham, "Is anything too hard for the LORD?"

Genesis 18:14 GNT

No eye has seen, no ear has heard, no mind has known what God has prepared for those who love him.

1 Corinthians 2:9 NIRV

One night the Lord spoke to Paul in a vision: "Do not be afraid; keep on speaking, do not be silent. For I am with you."

Acts 18:9–10 NIV

O Lord, this is our desire, to walk along the path of life that you have appointed us, in steadfastness of faith, in lowliness of heart, in gentleness of love.

—MARIA HARE

His Hand in Mine

A Moment to Pause   God is with you now. He is as near as your heartbeat, as close as your breath. Focus on God's presence. Be aware that he is there with you. Curl up in a large, comfy chair. Picture yourself as a child, snuggling with your perfect Father—one who will love you, protect you, cherish you, and hold you close, give you his strength, throughout eternity.

Relax in the comfort of his arms, almighty, yet tender. Picture yourself leaning against his powerful presence, moving ever so gently with the force of his own life-giving breath. Delight in his love for you. Take pleasure in his joy over the one-of-a-kind design he used to create you.

Imagine what it might be like to look up and come face to face with his glory. Speak to him—aloud, if you feel comfortable. Tell him how much it means to know he's near. Tell him how safe you feel, how grateful you are for his love. Whisper your secrets, even the ones you've never spoken aloud. Thank him for the difference his presence has made in your life.

Finish by sitting quietly. Listen for your father's still, small voice, speaking words of love meant for you alone.

Wait upon God and feel his good presence; this will
carry you evenly through your day's business.
—WILLIAM PENN

A Moment to Reflect

In the Old Testament, God's presence often came in a visible form, such as a cloud or a burning bush. After Moses spent time with God, those who saw him could tell something extraordinary had happened—his face glowed from getting just a glimpse of God.

Though God's presence seemed more dramatic—and tangible—in the Old Testament, it was also less accessible. It wasn't until God's gift of the Holy Spirit, as described in the story of Pentecost in the New Testament, that people were able to consistently experience God's presence in their life. As God's beloved daughter, celebrate that privilege often. Don't let a day go by without reminding yourself that God is near.

Let the sweet hope that thou art mine
my path of life attend;
Thy presence thro' my journey shine,
and crown my journey's end.

—ANNE STEELE

The LORD is near to all who call on him, to all who call on him in truth.

Psalm 145:18 NRSV

A Moment to Refresh

The LORD your God is with you, he is mighty to save. He will take great delight in you, he will quiet you with his love, he will rejoice over you with singing.

Zephaniah 3:17 NIV

As a mother comforts her child, so will I comfort you.

Isaiah 66:13 NIV

I always stay close to you, and you hold me by the hand.

Psalm 73:23 GNT

Rejoice in the Lord always. I will say it again: Rejoice! Let your gentleness be evident to all. The Lord is near.

Philippians 4:4–5 NIV

God is always near you and with you; leave Him not alone.

❧

—BROTHER LAWRENCE

I have stilled and quieted my soul; like a weaned child with its mother, like a weaned child is my soul within me.

Psalm 131:2 NIV

You have made known to me the ways of life; you will make me full of gladness with your presence.

Acts 2:28 NRSV

Draw near to God and He will draw near to you.

James 4:8 NASB

May the Lord strengthen your hearts so that you will be blameless and holy in the presence of our God and Father when our Lord Jesus comes with all his holy ones.

1 Thessalonians 3:13 NIV

[God] is not far away from us. Rather he awaits us every instant in our action, in the work of the moment. There is a sense in which he is at the tip of my pen, my spoke, my brush, my needle.

❧

—PIERRE TEILHARD
DE CHARDIN

At Inspirio we love to hear from you—your
stories, your feedback,
and your product ideas.
Please send your comments to us
by way of e-mail at
icares@zondervan.com
or to the address below:

inspirio

Attn: Inspirio Cares
5300 Patterson Avenue SE
Grand Rapids, MI 49530

If you would like further information
about Inspirio and the products we
create please visit us at:
www.inspiriogifts.com

Thank you and God Bless!